The EGYPTIANS

NEIL GRANT

MALLARD PRESS

Contents

Introduction	6
The River and the Desert	8
The Ancient Near East	8
The Nile	9
The Deserts	11
Everyday Life	12
Farming	12
Animals	14
Towns and Houses	16
Food and Drink	20
Families	22
Sports and Games	22
Government and Religion	23
Pharaoh	23
Government	24
The Gods	24
Death and Burial	27
Craftsmen and Merchants	29
Language and Writing	29
Mathematics and Science	29
Scribes	31
Other Crafts	31
Trade	32
Builders and Artists	34
Building Methods	34
The Pyramids	37
Labourers	38
Ships	40
Sculpture and Painting	41
Index	46

Introduction

Egyptian civilization lasted for nearly 3,000 years. That alone makes it almost unique in human history. It began about 3100 B.C. with the unification of Upper and Lower Egypt into one kingdom. The boundary between the two was never clearly defined, but it was somewhere about Memphis (near modern Cairo), which became the capital of the united kingdom. The First Cataract of the Nile, near Aswan, marked the approximate southern limit.

The event which marks the end of Ancient Egypt was the conquest by Alexander the Great in 332 B.C. The country lost its independence then, and never fully regained it until 1952.

At first sight, Egyptian civilization seems to have changed very little in all that time. Many ideas, customs and beliefs can be traced from the earliest to the latest times. But this impression of continuity is misleading. Every human society must change, even a society as conservative as Ancient Egypt.

Archaeologists have defined three main periods of Ancient Egypt: the Old Kingdom, the Middle Kingdom and the New Kingdom. The last of these is the period we know best. Together, these three periods make up less than half the total lifespan of Ancient Egypt. In between came many centuries when the kingdom was divided, government broke down, foreigners invaded, and many people died of starvation. For most of the two centuries before the invasion of Alexander the Great, Egypt was part of the Persian Empire. However, even through the worst times, Egyptian traditions and beliefs were maintained.

The history of Ancient Egypt is also divided up by dynasties, or ruling houses, of which altogether there were thirty (or perhaps thirty-one). This system was first established by Manetho, an Egyptian priest and historian who lived in the century after Alexander's conquest. However, it is often impossible to establish the exact dates of events, such as the death of a particular pharaoh (king). The dates in the following table are therefore approximate, and different dates will be found in other books.

Date	Dynasty	Period	Events
3100–2600	1–3	Early Dynastic Period	Formation of Egyptian civilization; little is known of this period.
2600–2160	4–8	Old Kingdom	First great period; pyramids built.
2160–2040	9–11	First Intermediate Period	Breakdown of central government.
2040–1700	11–13	Middle Kingdom	The kingdom reunited and prosperity restored.
1700–1570	14–17	Second Intermediate Period	Egypt overrun by Hyskos ("foreigners"); few records kept in this period.
1570–1070	18–20	New Kingdom	Reunited Egypt gained an Asian "empire" under the powerful 18th Dynasty.
1070–600	21–25	Third Intermediate Period	Break-up into small states.
600–332	26–30	Late Period	Egypt mainly under Persian rule.

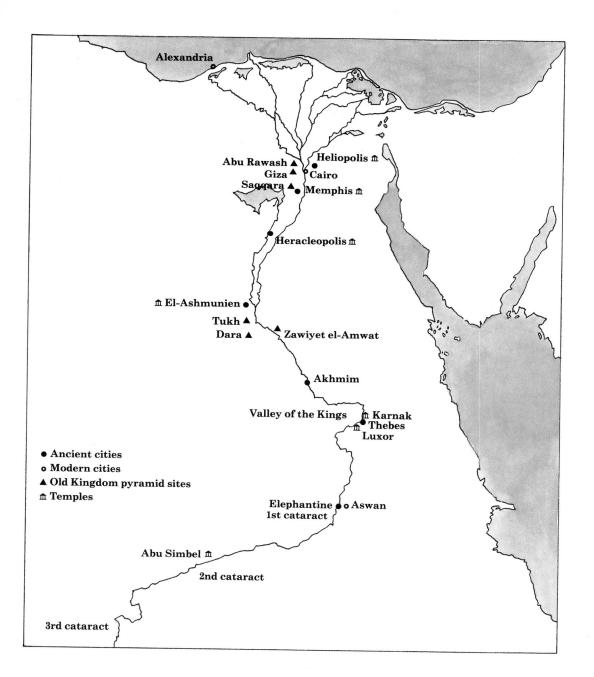

Alexandria

Abu Rawash ▲
Giza ▲
Saqqara ▲
Heliopolis 🏛
Cairo
Memphis 🏛

Heracleopolis 🏛

🏛 El-Ashmunien ●
Tukh ▲
Dara ▲ ▲ Zawiyet el-Amwat

Akhmim

Valley of the Kings 🏛 Karnak
Thebes
Luxor

● Ancient cities
○ Modern cities
▲ Old Kingdom pyramid sites
🏛 Temples

Elephantine ● ○ Aswan
1st cataract

Abu Simbel 🏛

2nd cataract

3rd cataract

Ancient Egypt was a strangely-shaped country, like a flower (the Delta) on a long stalk (the Nile Valley). Though narrow, it covered a large area as it was about 805 km (500 miles) from north to south.

The River and the Desert

The Ancient Near East

Egypt was not the only place that civilization was beginning 4,000 years ago. The first signs of it were present in the Far East – in China (the only civilization which rivalled Egypt in the length of time it lasted) and in India. In Mesopotamia (modern Iraq), developments were much more advanced. The Sumerians already had large stone buildings and a written language.

The main difference between Egypt and Mesopotamia was that Egypt was a national society. The whole country was ruled by a central government and the authority of the king, or pharaoh, was recognized throughout the land. Mesopotamia was still in the stage of city-states. No person or government ruled more than a small area; there was no "nation".

The god Horus (right), wearing the combined crown of upper and lower Egypt, and the cow goddess Hathor.

8

The Nile

Egypt is a very dry country. Not enough rain falls to grow crops, and without farming civilization cannot exist. What made it possible in Egypt was the River Nile.

The Nile runs from central Africa northward to the Mediterranean Sea. The main river is called the White Nile, which begins in Lake Victoria and flows steadily throughout the year. However, in former times, every summer the Nile overflowed its banks and covered the surface of the valley with mud and water. When the floodwaters went down, they left a rich, damp layer of silt. (Since the Aswan Dam was completed in 1972 this no longer happens.)

The annual flood was caused by the White Nile's two main tributaries, the Blue Nile and the smaller Atbara River, which carry water from the heavy winter rains in the mountains of Ethiopia. At the height of the flood, the amount of water increases to as much as 50 times the normal flow. This was enough to fertilize a strip of land along the course of the river which was as much as 40 km wide in some places (though much narrower in others).

In the Delta, where the river divided into seven branches (only two nowadays), it flooded a wide area – about $15,000 \text{ km}^2$ (5792 sq. miles). The layers of silt, built up by the flood year after year, were many metres deep, and so fertile that sometimes two or three crops could be grown in one year.

Ancient Egypt's greatest wealth was not its shining pyramids, not its great stone statues nor its golden crowns. Its greatest wealth was its soil. The Nile was truly the "mother" of Egyptian civilization.

The river also dictated the borders of the country since everyone lived in that narrow, fertile band along the valley. Except in the Delta, which was a wilder region in ancient times, infested by hippos and crocodiles, the desert was always close by. If you walked away from the river, you would reach it within a few hours at most.

Most movement in Egypt was therefore north and south, for the river was also the main highway. By a lucky chance the dominant wind is northerly. Boats going north drifted with the current. Going south, against the flow, they had the wind to help them.

The flooding of the Nile was the most important event of the year. The Egyptians organized their life around it, dividing the year into three seasons – Flood, Seed and Harvest. Life itself depended on the flood. In good years, people grew fat. In bad years, when the river was low, they went hungry.

During peaceful times the river was crowded with boats. Government officials travelled to and fro on business; raft-like boats carried produce, and ferries took people back and forth, from one side to the other. The ferrymen were often accused of overcharging, but the government officials, demanding taxes, were even less popular.

In the height of the flood season, about September, much of the country looked like one great lake. Villages became islands, protected against the water by banks or dykes. People could only get about by boat, or on raised roadways running along the canals. These were built for irrigation, bringing water to the fields once the flood had gone down, though in about 600 B.C. a much larger canal was built, from the Delta to the tip of the Red Sea at Suez – an early forerunner of the present Suez Canal.

The Nile is still the main highway and lifeline of Egypt.

In some parts of the country the fertile land consisted of a narrow strip by the River Nile hemmed in by lime cliffs. Beyond the cliffs lay the desert.

10

The Deserts

Although Ancient Egypt could be (and was) invaded, it would not have lasted so long if it had not been well guarded by nature. It was thanks to its geographical situation that Egyptian civilization developed almost without any foreign influence.

On both sides of the Nile Valley lay the desert. There, no settled life was possible, and invading armies could not cross the barren ground. In this respect Egypt was much luckier than Mesopotamia, which could be attacked from all sides.

In the south lay Nubia, inhabited by a darker-skinned people who were not so advanced as the Egyptians. They were no great threat, and Nubia eventually became an Egyptian colony.

The main danger lay in attacks from the sea, which helped to bring the New Kingdom to an end. However, for many, many centuries, Egypt was never threatened by hostile attack from outside its borders.

The deserts – even the great western desert of Libya – were not quite empty. The Egyptians were in contact with people who lived in the oases, and through them carried on trade with West Africa. They had other trade links with Mediterranean countries, and of course with Nubia, via the Nile.

But very few Egyptians ever visited these lands. For most of them, the world was a small place which stretched no farther than the fringes of the desert and the First Cataract of the Nile. Beyond that, the Egyptians said, lay "plains and hill countries, the foreign lands that know not Egypt".

Although the Egyptians regarded the Nubians as inferiors, in the 8th–9th century B.C. Egypt's power had waned and the country was briefly ruled by Nubian Kings.

Everyday Life

Farming

Ancient Egypt appears to us, at first, as a land of towering pyramids and splendid temples, of glittering treasure and god-like pharaohs. For the ordinary people, however, these were *not* the most important things in life.

The chief business of Egypt was farming, and in the paintings found in tombs, which often illustrate scenes of everyday life, among the most common subjects are sowing the seed and reaping the harvest.

Grain was the main crop, especially wheat – a primitive form of the wheat we grow today – and barley. From grain came the most basic foodstuff, bread, while barley was used to make beer, the Egyptians being great beer drinkers. Grain was the basis of the whole economy. As the Egyptians did not use cash, taxes were paid in corn. So were the wages of government officials and workers.

The land of Egypt was supposed to belong to the pharaoh, and a large part was farmed for him directly. In practice, there were other big landowners, of which the temples were the richest. Temples sometimes owned property in distant parts of the

Government men measuring the size of the crop to calculate the amount due in tax. In a bad year, that might turn out to be as much as half the crop.

Gathering the harvest. The harvest, if it were a good one, was a festive time in ancient Egypt. Men went out at dawn to cut the corn with sickles and worked until sunset, with a break at the hottest time of day.

country, as well as in their own district. During the 18th Dynasty, the Temple of Amun at Thebes owned about 10 per cent of all the farmland in Egypt.

Ordinary people could also own land, but most peasant farmers did not. Some were tenants, paying rent (in corn) for their plots. Others were paid workers on the farms of the big landowners.

Seed was sown after the floodwaters had gone down, when the fields had dried out enough to be ploughed. The plough did not cut and turn the soil in chunks, like a modern ploughshare. It was basically a heavy spike, pulled by oxen and guided by a man, which scored a furrow in the soil. The ground was sometimes broken up before ploughing by men with heavy mallets. Others marked out the furrows for the plough with hoes.

The seed was sown in the furrows made by the plough and covered over. Animals such as sheep or cattle might be driven across the soil to trample the seed into the ground and stop it being blown away.

The crop was harvested the following spring. The first people on the scene were the tax men, who calculated the size of the crop and the amount due in tax. The tax was heavy, and peasants who could not pay received little mercy: they were lucky to escape with a beating.

The reapers cut the ripe corn with sickles, while women and children gleaned what was left. The grain was carried in baskets slung on poles from the fields to the threshing floor, where it was trodden by donkeys or oxen to separate grain from chaff. Women did the winnowing, scooping up the trodden grain and tossing it into the air, so the chaff was blown away while the heavier grain fell to the ground. Finally, it was carried to the granaries, and stored in silos.

13

Another big crop was flax. This is not a food crop, but the plant from which linen is made. Thanks to the climate, the Egyptians did not need to wear a lot of clothes for most of the time, but those they did wear were usually made of linen. It was woven into a very light cloth, sometimes so fine it was transparent.

The Egyptians grew a large variety of vegetables and fruit. Onions, lettuces, radishes, beans, turnips and gourds were raised in garden plots; figs, dates, pomegranates and melons in orchards. Oranges and lemons were not known, but there were many vineyards, where the vines were trained to grow on pergolas.

In addition to their liking for beer, the Egyptians also made wine. The grapes were first trampled by human feet in troughs. Sometimes a musician played and the tramplers stamped to the music. The juice was strained into buckets, then through a linen bag and poured into jars sealed with a clay stopper.

The Egyptians may have been the first people for whom gardening was also a hobby. In the gardens of rich men, besides the vines, fruit and vegetables, flowers also grew.

They were certainly the first people to use irrigation – artificial watering. They dug small canals linked to the Nile, and stored water in basins. They also dug wells. Some crops had to be watered every day which meant a lot of hard work even with canals and wells. During the New Kingdom, the Egyptians invented a machine to make the job easier. This was the *shaduf* (its Arabic name), and it is still used today in some country districts. It worked on the principle of a lever. A pole was attached to a raised crosspiece with a bucket hung from one end and a weight at the other to balance it. Where the river bank was high two or three *shadufs* might be placed one above the other, carrying water to the higher level of the fields.

Animals

Farm animals were no less important than crops. Herds of cows provided milk, as well as meat. Flocks of sheep and goats were also kept, and pigs too, although pork was regarded as inferior meat, not to be eaten by respectable persons. Pork was, of course, also forbidden among the Israelites of the Old Testament, and there may be a practical reason behind this ancient bias against pig meat. In a hot climate, meat goes bad rather quickly, and food poisoning is more likely from bad pork than from beef or mutton.

The Egyptians also disliked fish, although the Nile was full of them. As with pork, fish was eaten by poor people because they could not get anything better. In times of famine, naturally, people ate anything they could get.

Chickens were unknown in Ancient Egypt until a late date, yet the Egyptians ate plenty of fowl. They kept ducks and

Irrigation channels helped to produce good crops in the Nile valley, as detailed in this wall painting from the Tomb of Sennejem.

Herdsmen with cattle, from a tomb painting of the New Kingdom. As in other ancient societies, cattle were a symbol of wealth.

geese, as well as pigeons, and, among the rich at least, wildfowl were on the menu at any banquet. A net was used to capture wildfowl in the marshy Delta, where they gathered in huge flocks.

The pictures of farming in tomb paintings show that the Egyptians looked after their animals with great care. We see them helping sheep and goats escape from thorny scrub, assisting cows giving birth, branding animals with their owner's name, and persuading cattle to ford the river by pulling a calf ahead of them. (The cows were quite right to be nervous as the Nile then contained many more crocodiles than it does today.)

That the Egyptians really liked animals is clear from the pictures we see of their

pets. The cat held a special position in Ancient Egypt, but they also kept pet dogs, monkeys and other animals. They were remarkably good at training them. Dogs were used in hunting, but cats too were trained to retrieve birds. Tame monkeys were taught to pick figs.

Towns and Houses

Although some of Egypt's grandest buildings have survived for an amazing length of time, ordinary houses, villages and even whole cities have disappeared almost without trace. One reason is that the houses of ordinary people were not built of stone, like the temples and palaces, but of mud bricks.

Bricks were made to a standard size in a

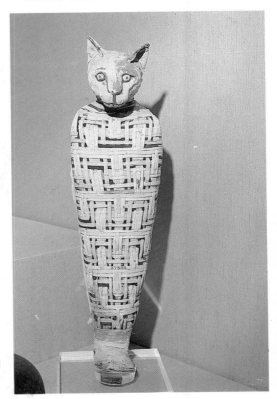

mould, out of wet mud strengthened with straw chopped up fine, and were put out to dry in the sun until they were hard. Mud-brick buildings would never have done in northern Europe, but in Egypt's dry climate they lasted a long time, though not for thousands of years. Old houses were also raided for their bricks which, crumbled up, made good fertilizer.

We imagine Egyptian towns consisting of grand stone buildings standing in splendid isolation. In reality, the buildings were often surrounded by a mass of scruffy huts and shelters. Now and then an official would order a general "slum clearance", but the lean-tos and mud huts soon crept back.

Ancient Egypt was heavily populated, supporting perhaps four or five million people – a huge number for those days. However, cities, in our sense of the word, developed late in Egypt, which always remained a farming country (as it largely is today). By the time of Alexander's conquest, there were nearly 200 cities in the Delta alone, but by modern standards they were very small towns.

They often grew up around a religious centre, a place devoted to the worship of a local god. Memphis, the first capital of a united Egypt, was the home of the god Ptah. Abydos was the site of the impressive ceremonies associated with Osiris. Thebes, the greatest city of the New Kingdom, was made up largely of temples and palaces, with the huge temples of Karnak and Luxor

Opposite: Geese, from a tomb painting at Thebes, which shows how closely the artist observed his subject. These geese are a good example of how animals were shown in a more natural way than human beings.

Opposite, below left: A nobleman hunting wildfowl with a throwing stick, helped by a hunting cat which is jumping to grasp falling birds. Such figures are often shown with a girl – perhaps a daughter – holding the hunter's leg as if to stop him falling off his papyrus boat. This girl is plucking a lotus flower.

Opposite, below right: Cats held a special place among the Egyptians, because they were identified with the cat-goddess, Bast (she was originally a lioness). This mummy of a cat was encased in a bronze coffin.

The ruins of the town of Deir el Medina.

17

close by on the other side of the river.

The houses of ordinary people, even quite wealthy ones, were plain in appearance. They were enclosed by a high wall and had stairs up to a flat roof. People spent a lot of time on the roof, as the inside was gloomy. The only "windows" (no glass) were very small and set high in the walls. In Egypt, because of the heat, houses are designed to keep sunlight out, not to let it in.

Grander houses too, looked plain and box-like from the outside, but they were much more comfortable. They stood among well-stocked gardens, with a pool for waterfowl and a small religious shrine. Steps led up to the front entrance which opened into a large hall, with two rows of columns. Beyond the hall was the main living room and dining room, a spacious chamber, again with columns, and a high ceiling. From the outside the house looked as if it was built on two levels. At one end of this room was a raised platform, on which people lounged among cushions and rugs.

Smaller rooms were ranged all around, including the main bedroom, offices, larders and rooms for the higher-ranking servants. Other servants slept in separate buildings, among stables and storehouses. The kitchen was also separate, perhaps to keep smells away.

The main rooms were decorated with paintings, tiles or wooden panels (wood was scarce, and when an owner moved house he took his wood panels and columns with him). Furniture was sparse, mainly chairs, beds or couches, low tables, stools

Modern Egyptian
houses of mud-brick
are little different
from those of ancient
times.

and chests for storage.

Some marvellous furniture has been found in royal tombs. Egyptian cabinet makers were excellent craftsmen, and Egyptian style, which changed very little between the Old and New Kingdoms, was distinctive and attractive. It became extremely popular in Europe at the beginning of the 19th century, after Napoleon's expedition to Egypt. The Ancient Egyptians were responsible, for example, for the lion's-paw feet on chairs, for X-shaped folding stools, for interlocking leather straps to make chair seats, and many other features which we see in European furniture of the past 200 years.

The finest furniture, with beautiful veneers, inlaid gold and enamel, was made for royal palaces. Poor people, on the other hand, had almost no furniture. They made do with sleeping mats and perhaps a rough table. Even rich people often sat on the floor.

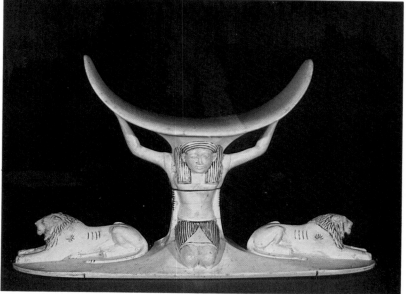

Food and Drink

The Egyptians enjoyed food, and wealthy people ate very well. They liked meat best, especially beef, although they also ate mutton and goat and the meat of wild animals like gazelles, which they hunted in the desert. Milk, butter and eggs (though not chicken eggs) were in good supply, and Egyptian bakers made many kinds of bread and cake. Salads of lettuce and cucumber were popular, and were probably eaten with oil and vinegar dressing, though it was not olive oil as the Ancient Egyptians did not grow olives. Nor did they have sugar, but they kept bees for their honey to sweeten food.

Food and drink were served in earthenware vessels. These were often beautiful, the slender wine jars especially. As they did

Banquets were the Egyptians' chief form of entertainment and relaxation. They were livened up by pretty girls who performed as musicians, dancers, and acrobats, and served the food and wine.

20

A trio of girl musicians, from a tomb painting. The Egyptians had what would now be called stringed, woodwind and brass instruments.

not have forks or spoons, the Egyptians ate with their fingers. Servants were on hand with bowls and jugs of water for rinsing greasy hands. However, the Egyptians did not mind being a little greasy. At banquets, lumps of scented fat were placed on a guest's head, to melt slowly, annointing him with sweet-smelling oil.

Among the rich, banquets were frequent.

Besides the food and drink, entertainment was provided by girl dancers, acrobats and musicians, who played many kinds of instrument including early versions of the harp. Jugglers and clowns, often dwarfs, helped keep the guests amused.

Poor people probably ate meat (beef anyway) very seldom, and fish more often. Their main diet was bread and vegetables.

Families

Family life was important to the Egyptians. Although the husband was the boss, marriage was a true partnership. Egyptian paintings often show affection between husband and wife – the man with his arm around the woman, for example – and this is uncommon in the art of other early civilizations.

However, rich men could have more than one wife. The pharaoh had a harem of wives, including foreign princesses sent to be his brides. Still, the chief wife was a person who commanded respect. She ran the household, and she was the legal owner of the household goods. It was not thought wrong for a husband to beat his wife, as long as he was not really cruel. Children too suffered corporal punishment. "A boy's ears are in his backside," said one tutor.

This did not mean that the Egyptians disliked children. On the contrary, they seem to have cherished them with great affection.

Sports and Games

Although we cannot tell what the rules were exactly, many games were played in Ancient Egypt – by adults as well as children. In the British Museum are balls made of wood, or of feathers covered in leather, which were the playthings of Egyptian children 4,000 years ago. Some girls' dolls have also survived, and paintings show young people playing leapfrog and a game like hopscotch.

Boys were encouraged to practise more "manly" sports, such as wrestling and archery. At an early age boys took part in hunting, the chief sport of rich Egyptian men. It required some skill to bring down a wild duck or quail with a throwing stick (which worked something like a boomerang), and some courage to spear a hippo from a small boat made of reeds.

Board games were also very popular. Dice, ivory figurines and wooden gaming boards have been found in tombs.

A wooden game, with drawers for the counters, from the 19th Dynasty. The rules unfortunately are a mystery.

Government and Religion

Pharaoh

The Egyptians, unlike people today, did not expect life to get better in the future; they believed it had been better in the past. Once there had been a golden age, when the gods had lived on earth and reigned over Egypt. People felt a desire to recapture that golden age, and one reason why the Egyptians did not welcome change was that any change took them farther away from this mythical past, which was enshrined in their traditions.

The most powerful of those traditions was that of divine kingship. The pharaoh was not only a king, he was also a god. He was particularly identified with the falcon-god Horus, son of Ra the sun god, though he was also an incarnation of Ra himself. When he died, he became Osiris, the god of the dead. Or, to be more exact, he became *an* Osiris.

The divinity of the pharaoh was altogether rather complicated, but what mattered was that he was a figure of immense holiness, and his authority was absolute. He was both the political and religious head, and all power in the kingdom, from the lowest tax collector to the highest priest, belonged finally to him. Right and wrong could be defined as "what Pharaoh approves of" and "what Pharaoh disapproves of".

His life was a constant succession of

The crowns of Upper Egypt (left) and Lower Egypt (right), from carved reliefs at Dendara.

Opposite, top: The head of the God Amun, from a statue. He wears the false beard seen on other statues of pharaohs and gods.

Opposite, right: Gold figure of the god Ptah. He came from Memphis and was an important national god in the Old Kingdom.

rituals. For example, like other men, he had a bath first thing in the morning. But the pharaoh's bath was no ordinary wash and brush-up. It was a ceremonial cleaning, performed in a temple, the purpose of which was to restore vigour to the kingdom and give it strength for the new day. Other ceremonies followed. The whole business of life in Egypt was thought to depend on these ceremonies carried out by the pharaoh with the aid of priests.

Every little incident was heavy with meaning. It was considered fearful bad luck if the pharaoh's shadow happened to fall on you; to be allowed to kiss his foot was a tremendous honour. The pharaoh's power was enormous, but his personal life was dreadfully limited. Being a god has its drawbacks.

Government

In modern terms, Egypt was a bureaucratic society; it was governed – and on the whole efficiently governed – by a large number of civil servants. There was an official in charge of everything, and there were so many ranks and titles that it is often difficult to understand exactly what duties were involved. Was the Superintendent of the Double Bathroom a glorified cleaner, or was this just a title of honour, like a Commander of the Order of the Bath in England?

The most important person after the pharaoh was the chief minister or vizier. Sometimes this was a title of honour too, given to a prince of the royal family. But we do know about several viziers, like Imhotep in the Old Kingdom, who were such effective "prime ministers" that in later times they too were regarded as gods.

Among his many duties, the vizier acted as a kind of appeal judge, deciding legal arguments which could not be decided at a lower level. He also kept an eye on tax returns, on the stock in the royal warehouses, on water supply and many other matters. He dealt with questions raised by local officials and interviewed foreign ambassadors.

Among his trickiest tasks was dealing with the rulers of the provinces, called *nomes*. They were noblemen who held considerable power in their own part of the country and, in times of weak central government, acted as independent princes. They were also inclined to quarrel among themselves, with disastrous effects on the country as a whole.

The Gods

Besides the aristocracy and the higher-ranking civil servants, the most powerful group in the country was the priests.

As in other early civilizations, it is impossible to separate Egyptian religion from other aspects of society, such as politics or economics. Temples, for example, were not only buildings for religious ceremonies; they were also schools, libraries, storehouses and workshops. They stood at the centre of the economic and social life of the people. Priests, like monks in Christian or Buddhist countries, were involved in ordinary work besides their religious duties.

The religion of Ancient Egypt seems strange, almost grotesque, to us. That is partly because we find it difficult to put ourselves in the place of the people who worshipped such strange – and so many (about 700) – gods and goddesses.

The main purpose of religion is to explain the meaning of life, and in ancient times, when scientific causes of things were entirely unknown, religion had a great deal to explain. The gods were numerous, strange and frightening (or amusing) because life was like that.

To begin with, there were local gods. Amun-Ra, who became the chief god, resulted from a merger of the Theban god Amun and the sun god Ra from Heliopolis. Other towns had their own versions of him, merged with their own local god. All these local gods and goddesses, and local religious traditions, make Egyptian religion

24

rather complicated.

The world was created, according to Egyptian belief, by Atum, who became the sun god Ra, who produced the Earth (Geb) and the Sky (Nut, sister and also wife of Geb). The worship of Ra and his varieties, especially Amun-Ra, became the most widespread in Egypt, although that did not prevent other gods being worshipped as well.

Among the chief gods who became more important in later times were the divine family of Osiris, his wife Isis and his brother Seth, a sinister god. Osiris was murdered by Seth, but Isis put him back together again and he became the god of the underworld. Horus, son of Osiris and Isis, defeated Seth and became ruler of earth (hence his identification with the pharaoh).

Other widely respected gods were Ptah, god of craftsmen and the chief god in the Old Kingdom, Hathor, the cow-goddess of music and pleasure, Thoth, the ibis-headed god of wisdom, and Anubis, the jackal-headed god of death and the tomb. The animal heads were a sign of the Egyptians' respect for the whole of Nature, and sacred animals of the kind identified with an individual god were kept in his temple. For example, a sacred crocodile lived in the precincts of the temple of Sebek, the crocodile-headed god.

The gods were worshipped and received sacrifices in their temples. The purpose was to ensure that they would maintain harmony and security. Some ceremonies were highly elaborate: the annual festival of Amun, when the images of the god and his family were carried by water from Karnak to Luxor, lasted for a month. It was held in the Flood season when there was no work to be done in the fields.

In spite of these lengthy rituals, however, Egyptian religion has no great body of teaching attached to it. It had no sacred book, no Bible or Koran. In some ways the gods were treated as if they were ordinary people. Many stories, some of them humorous, were told about their family troubles. And if a local god failed to perform some request put to him, he might be "punished" by being given no offerings for a time. It was not unknown for disappointed worshippers to give the image or statue of the god a good beating!

Death and Burial

Religious ceremonies included feasting, dancing and good times. But Egyptian religion also had its grim side, in its intense concern with death.

The Egyptians believed that after a person died, he would go to a kind of heavenly Egypt somewhere "in the West". However, many ceremonies had to be performed for this to happen.

The dead person's tomb was his "home" and had to be looked after by priests who spent their lives in the service of the dead. Every day they said prayers, provided daily offerings of food, and kept guard over the treasure and household goods which were buried with the dead man in case he needed them in the next world.

The tombs of pharaohs and noblemen became large underground buildings – palaces of the dead – with courtyards and porches, halls, chapels and other rooms, besides the burial chamber itself. Some were magnificently decorated with paintings and sculpture in relief.

Probably the greatest archaeological discovery of this century was the tomb of the 18th-Dynasty pharaoh Tutankamun in 1922 – the only royal Egyptian tomb which had not been wrecked by robbers or vandals. It contained marvellous treasures – a throne, weapons and a chariot, and furniture decorated with gold and ivory – as well as the coffin containing the mummy of the pharaoh himself.

By that time "mummification" (preserving a dead body), as practised by the priests of Anubis, had become a fine art. It was done like this:

First, the inner organs were removed. The brain was extracted through the nostrils, to leave the head undamaged, and the intestines removed through a cut in the stomach. The heart was wrapped and replaced in the body: it was believed to be the organ of the intelligence and feelings, and would therefore be needed in the afterlife. The other organs were placed in special jars which were placed in the tomb along with the mummy.

The empty interior of the body was packed with sawdust and spices, and the body dried in natron, a kind of soda which the Egyptians acquired by trade with certain desert oases.

The drying process took about 70 days. Then the body was washed and oiled and wrapped tightly in linen bandages. Each finger and toe was bandaged separately. Tutankamun was wrapped in no less than sixteen layers. Sometimes, false eyes were inserted, and a kind of resin was rubbed into the skin, making it look plump and alive.

The funeral could now take place, with the mummy carried to the tomb on a sledge. It was encased in a stone coffin, often beautifully sculpted, and in some periods the mummy was provided with a beautifully painted mask in the likeness of the dead person.

The gold coffin of Tutankamun, which contained the mummified pharaoh. It was itself contained in another coffin, made of stone.

The Rosetta Stone, now in the British Museum, which led to an understanding of hieroglyphics.

The mummy of Tutankamun was placed in three coffins, the innermost one being solid gold. His death mask was also gold. In another chamber of the tomb were the jars containing the intestines. These were called Canopic vases, after the Egyptian city Canopus, and were in a chest made of marble which was itself contained in a shrine of gold-painted wood. There were also models of ships, a bakery and brewery, for the pharaoh's use in the next world. Nothing was forgotten.

Craftsmen, Clerks and Merchants

Language and Writing

The art of writing was probably invented in Sumeria, but the Egyptians soon produced their own writing in the form of hieroglyphics – signs or little pictures which represent either sounds or things. Apart from being difficult to learn (there were hundreds of different signs, and many of them could mean different things depending on the context), it was also very slow to write. In time a more cursive, or flowing, form of writing developed, based on the original hieroglyphics. This form is known as hieratic. In the Late Period, another cursive text, called demotic, also came into use. This was used by the laity and the common people, though hieroglyphics were never abandoned. Hieratic was used in business letters and literature, the hieroglyphic system for inscriptions.

After Alexander's conquest in 332 B.C., Greek became the language of the civilized world. Although it took a long time to disappear completely, all knowledge of the Egyptian language was eventually lost. When Europeans came to investigate Ancient Egypt in the 18th century, the language was to them a meaningless code; they could not understand one word.

In 1799 some French soldiers in Rosetta, Egypt, looking for stones to strengthen their forts against the British, discovered what became known as the Rosetta Stone. This was a large stone slab bearing a long inscription in three languages. The first was in hieroglyphics, the second in demotic, and the third was – *in Greek*! From this clue, the texts of ancient Egypt were eventually deciphered.

The Egyptians, like all bureaucratic societies, liked to keep written records of everything (for which historians are extremely grateful). The "paper" they used came from the papyrus plant, a type of reed which then (though not now) grew widely in Egypt. In fact this useful plant has many purposes: quite large boats were made of it, for example.

To make it into sheets for writing, the outside of the stalk was stripped off and the inner pith sliced into thin strips. The strips were laid out flat, edges overlapping, in two layers, one at right angles to the other. When they were pressed or hammered together, the juice which was squeezed out bound the strips together, and the end result was a smooth sheet. The Egyptian "pen" was a fine brush, made from the stem of a reed. Black ink was made from carbon, red ink from red ochre (a form of iron ore).

Mathematics and Science

The Egyptians were a practical people: they were perhaps better at doing things than thinking about them in an abstract way. For that reason their system of mathematics was rather clumsy. This was one area of knowledge where Mesopotamia was ahead of Egypt.

The only signs for numbers were 1 and multiples of 10. The number 132, for example, was therefore written as $100 + 10 + 10 + 10 + 1 + 1$. Such a system made multiplying and dividing a wearisome business. The Egyptians did have the abacus to help them make calculations, and they also had a good understanding of geometry – as anyone might guess after looking at the pyramids.

The Egyptians were probably the first people to measure time with a high degree of accuracy. It was important for them to know when annual changes like the flooding of the Nile were due, and they soon learned to do this by observing the movements of the stars.

Their calendar was based on the Moon, and divided into months. However, twelve lunar months do not make one year, so the Egyptians devised a calendar of twelve 30-day months plus five extra days – 365

days in all. That is as close as you can get in days but it is, as we know, roughly six hours too short. We get round that problem with an extra day every fourth or "leap" year, but the Egyptians never thought of that. As a result, their calendar went slowly but steadily wrong, so that after many centuries had passed, a festival which was supposed to take place in summer actually occurred in winter.

Considering their amazing skill in mummification, the Egyptians understood less about the human body than might be expected. Their medical practice was largely a matter of magic spells. As in other areas of life, religious customs and beliefs dictated their ideas on medicine and science.

However, Egyptian medicine was famous in the ancient world, and in some matters they showed surprising knowledge. They practised some primitive dentistry, and they were very good at mending broken bones. Pictures of a surgical operation appear in some tombs, although it is difficult to tell what it is – or if it was successful!

Scribes

In the scenes of everyday life found in the tombs, scribes, or clerks, appear very frequently, keeping records of production, taxes, trade, punishments and many other activities. The scribes were the managers and supervisors of Ancient Egypt as well as the clerks, and like other trades, their craft was usually hereditary.

Training to be a scribe was hard, if only because of the number of signs which had to be learned. Boys were sent to special schools, where they lived in dormitories and got up with the dawn to begin their lessons. By the age of twelve, a boy had learned enough to go out to work as a junior scribe.

The fact that scribes were rather unpopular was partly due, no doubt, to envy. They had important, secure and well-paid jobs,

which did not require any hard, physical labour. "Be a scribe," one teacher said to his pupils, "so that your limbs may grow smooth and your hands soft."

Other Crafts

Probably most Egyptians could not read or write. At a very early age boys started to learn, but what they learned was their father's trade. For many trades, reading

Above: A 5th Dynasty scribe called Accroupi recording government statistics.

Opposite: The pyramids of the 4th-Dynasty pharaohs at Giza, near Cairo.

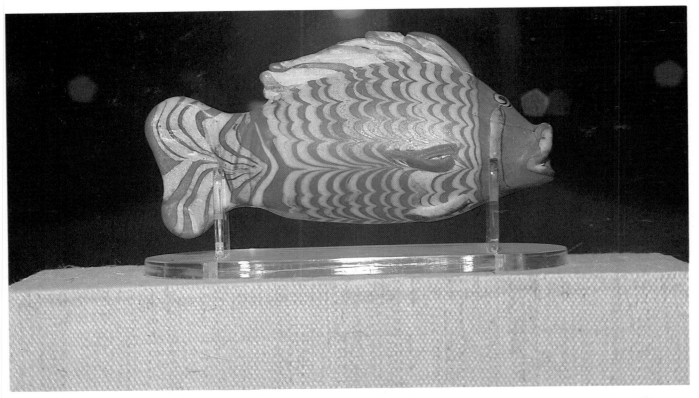

A coloured glass
vessel in the shape of
a fish, made during the
18th Dynasty.

and writing were not necessary.

Among the most skilful workers in
Ancient Egypt were carpenters and, as we
would call them cabinet makers. The best
furniture was of high quality in both design
and construction.

Potters and glass makers were equally
skilled. Although the Egyptians did not dis-
cover the trick of blowing glass, they made
beautiful glass vessels by coiling strips of
coloured glass, while it was hot and pliable,
around a core of clay. One fine example of a
glass vase is made of zig-zag strips of different colours and is in the perfect form of a
fish.

Egypt did not have to fight many wars,
but it did have an army. The soldiers' main
job was to guard the frontiers, especially to

the east of the Delta, and to keep the peace
inside the kingdom. When Egypt did have
to fight major wars, most of the troops were
mercenaries – hired foreigners – from
Nubia or the countries of the eastern Mediterranean.

Trade

The rich country of Egypt provided its
people with most of the necessities of life,
but some things had to be obtained from
foreign lands. Wood, for example, was hard
to find in Egypt where few trees grew, and
cedarwood had to be imported from the
Lebanon. Gold and other valuable minerals
were obtained through the desert oases and
Nubia, copper from the Sinai Desert.

The Egyptians ventured south through Nubia and south-west to Darfur more than 2,000 years before the birth of Jesus. On one recorded expedition they reached Darfur by the Forty Days road, which leaves the Nile near Aswan, and brought back ebony, ivory and frankincense, as well as a "dancing dwarf" – perhaps a pygmy. Their caravan consisted of 300 donkeys, a third of them carrying water for the journey.

Some three or four centuries after that expedition, we hear of a famous voyage to the land of Punt (probably modern Somalia), which was reached by sailing down the Red Sea to the East African coast. The Egyptians had to cross the desert to the Red Sea, and they built their boats when they arrived at the coast. A description of this voyage, which was the first of many, still exists, carved on a stone slab.

This took place during the reign of Queen Hatshepsut of the 18th Dynasty, who reigned as regent for her nephew Thutmose III, and later in her own right with full powers of the pharaoh. The greatest monument of her reign was a beautiful temple at Thebes where, among other scenes, the voyage to Punt is shown in relief sculpture. It is a lively scene, with baboons hopping about in the rigging of the ships. Among the goods being loaded at Punt are sacks of myrrh (incense, probably the main object of the expedition), ebony, ivory, gold, sweet-smelling woods, dogs and monkeys, leopard skins (much admired in Egypt) and even whole trees, their roots protected by baskets. In exchange, the Egyptians traded beads, bracelets and weapons.

The reliefs of the Punt expedition are very informative about that country, even though we cannot tell exactly where it was. The native plants, animals and people are carefully pictured. It is obvious that the Egyptians, while convinced that they were superior to other people, had what we would call a genuine scientific interest in other lands.

In Egypt itself, buying and selling in the markets was, as it still is, a matter of hard bargaining. As there was no money, the value of any goods depended on what a buyer was prepared to trade in exchange. Painted scenes of fairs and markets show a lot of haggling going on.

Left and below: Scenes illustrating the expedition to Punt, from the Temple of Queen Hatshepsut.

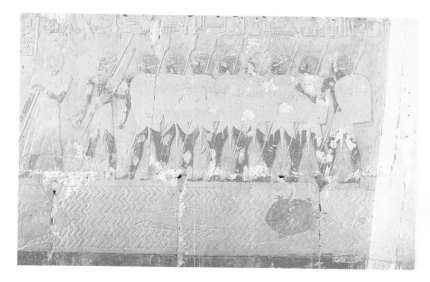

Builders and Artists

Building Methods

The most obvious evidence of their civilization left by the Egyptians is their huge buildings – tombs, palaces and, above all, the pyramids. Though they had only simple equipment and basic methods, they nevertheless erected buildings which would be remarkable enough if they had the benefit of all the resources of modern technology.

Egyptian architecture is not especially beautiful to our eyes, although it is certainly impressive. It is what is called monumental architecture: it makes an impression not of grace or elegance, but of mighty power. Some details of decoration, like capitals of columns carved in the form of plants, are pleasing, but as a whole the buildings do not give us a sense of delight. The great Egyptian buildings are huge, squarish and tremendously solid. No one can look at them without feeling great respect for the builders, who placed such importance on survival. Nothing made by man lasts for ever, but the buildings of the Egyptians are the most successful so far.

In building, as in other aspects of life, the Egyptians remained sternly loyal to their traditions. One drawback of their dedication to the old ways was that, not only was there no "progress", a word which would have meant nothing to them, but they sometimes failed to learn from their own mistakes. Buildings of the Old Kingdom were sometimes built on poor foundations, and in many places that did not matter because the ground was so hard. Sometimes it did matter, yet we find signs of the same fault in buildings of the New Kingdom, a thousand years later.

Unlike the brick houses, monumental buildings were built of stone. In the days of the pyramids, it was usually limestone from the quarries of Tura, not far from modern Cairo. In the New Kingdom, the pharaohs preferred to use sandstone, from quarries on either side of the river north of Aswan. The famous temples of Karnak and Luxor are built of this material. Granite was also available, and was sometimes used as a facing on temples. But it was not easily cut by people who did not have iron or steel tools.

Limestone and sandstone could be cut quite easily with copper or bronze chisels, which were struck with a wooden mallet. To reach stone of the best quality the masons sank galleries that ran for hundreds of metres into the rock. They dug around the stone and split off large chunks with the aid of wooden wedges.

The stone was hauled to the river on wooden sledges. In some places raised road-

The colossal statues outside the Temple of Rameses II, Abu Simbel. They were moved out of the way of the new reservoir in the 1950s, a huge job which proved nearly as difficult as their construction must have been. The four figures of the pharaoh (one mostly destroyed) represent him as himself and as the three chief national gods of his time. Some of his children appear – tiny by him yet still much larger than life size – at his feet.

ways were specially built. It was a tremendous task. One obelisk, a pillar made from a single block, which was moved in this way, weighed over 1,117,600 kg (1,100 tons).

At the river the stone was loaded on to large barge-like boats, which were towed by smaller boats. When it reached its destination, it had to be hauled to the building site again. It is astonishing that the Egyptians were able to shift such heavy loads with no power except human muscle – though they did have a lot of that.

Once the raw material was in position, building could begin. Because the design contained nothing new or unusual, plans were probably not necessary, though they were used at times.

As the Egyptians had no pulleys or lifting tackle, the stones had to be raised via a ramp and levered into position with poles. Mortar of a kind was sometimes used, not so much to bind the blocks together as to adjust them to the right position. The pyramids were built by this method.

The Pyramids

The pyramids were tombs built to contain the bodies of the pharaohs. They developed from an earlier type of tomb called a *mastaba*, which was a low, flat-topped building with a burial chamber far below the ground. The first stone pyramid, built for Zoser, a pharaoh of the 3rd Dynasty, had sides that rose like steps, in six stages, to a height of 60 metres (65.6 yards). The true pyramid, with four smooth sides rising to a point, developed later.

The pyramid did not stand alone. It was part of a complex of buildings, temples and walled enclosures. Nearly 100 pyramids are known, but most of them are now no more than piles of rubble. The finest surviving pyramids are the group of three at Giza just outside modern Cairo (the city's suburbs have, unfortunately, almost reached them). These three were classed by the people of ancient times as one of the Seven Wonders of the World.

The largest, and oldest, of the three is the Great Pyramid of Khufu (or Cheops), a pharaoh of the 4th Dynasty. Its base is almost a perfect square, 230 metres (251.5 yards) along each side, and it covered an area of about 5.3 hectares (13 acres). The five largest cathedrals in Europe could all be placed within that space. It contains about 2,300,000 blocks of stone which have an average weight of 2540 kg (2.5 tons).

This is probably the greatest single building ever constructed by men, yet it is about 4,500 years old! Although it is a breathtaking sight, it does not look quite as grand now as it did when it was first built. It is about twelve metres shorter and it has lost its smooth and glittering outer casing of fine limestone.

Pyramids continued to be built for many centuries, though not on such a scale as the Great Pyramid. The pharaohs of the New Kingdom, however, were buried in concealed tombs in the rocks. Pyramids had been abandoned altogether, at least for royal burials. Security was the main prob-

lem. Pyramids standing high above the desert were an invitation to robbers. In fact the only important royal tomb that was not stripped of its treasures long before archaeologists entered it was the tomb of Tutankamun. Even that had been entered not long after the pharaoh's death, but the thieves were caught and the contents replaced. Later, the tomb was covered by rubble from another tomb being built above it, and so remained hidden.

Above: The Sphinx at Giza was carved out of a huge limestone rock in the form of a lion with a human head, representing the Pharaoh Khafre.

Opposite: Massive figures range the interior of the Temple of Rameses II.

37

Labourers

The Egyptian substitute for cranes and lorries was human strength. In their great building projects they employed thousands of workers. Everyone was supposed to give their labour as a kind of tax, but in practice this meant just the peasants – the mass of the population – and not priests, scribes, officials or, of course, noblemen.

The division of the year into seasons was very helpful. At seed time and harvest, the peasants were busy in the fields. But during the four months of the flood they had little to do.

Besides ordinary Egyptian peasants, the pharaohs also employed slave labour. All ancient societies had slaves, and the Egyptians were no exception. There was nothing especially horrible about slavery then, when life for most people was much harder than it is now. However, it was not until the New Kingdom, long after the great age of the pyramids, that Egypt obtained a really big supply of slaves, as a result of their conquests in the Middle East and Nubia.

We know very little about the ordinary workers, whether slaves or native Egyptians. The Israelites of the Old Testament, during their exile in Egypt, seem to have been left alone most of the time, although they may well have been badly treated by Egyptian overseers.

Archaeologists have excavated several "towns" or settlements which were specially built for the workers on the grand buildings of the New Kingdom. The houses of the workmen were rather small compared with houses built for officials, but they had three or four rooms and were probably just as comfortable as the houses of the peasants in farming villages.

Labourers were paid in food and drink – bread, vegetables, dried fish and meat, and beer. Sometimes they might be given clothes, wine, or oil for using on the body and other "luxuries". Those who worked permanently on the building sites had a holiday every eleventh day and on religious festivals. On at least one occasion, when their pay failed to arrive on time, the labourers went on strike, demanding one month's pay before they went back to work. The strike was a success: the food arrived swiftly, the labourers returned to work and, surprisingly, no one was punished.

A plan of the Pyramid of Khafre (2558–2533 B.C.). On its final journey the royal corpse progressed from the valley temple where it was embalmed, through the causeway into the mortuary temple, before being laid in its tomb in the pyramid itself.

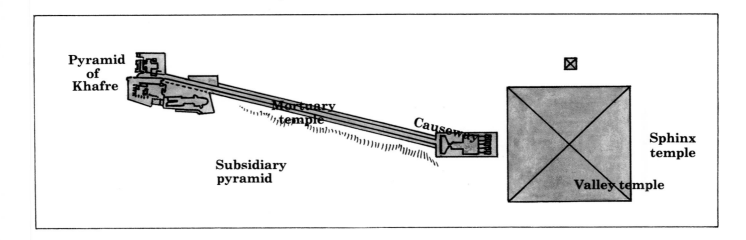

Pyramid of Khafre

Mortuary temple

Causeway

Subsidiary pyramid

Valley temple

Sphinx temple

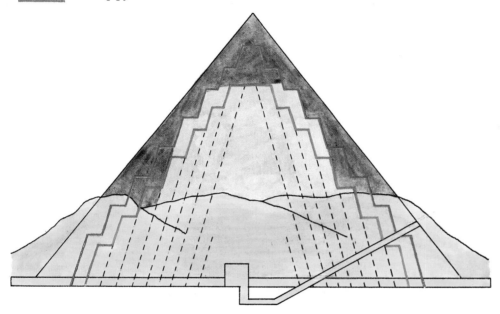

8-step pyramid

7-step pyramid

The earliest Egyptian rulers' tombs were flat-topped, bench-like structures called mastaba. In about 2650 B.C. the first pyramid-shaped tomb was built at Saqqara. This had stepped rather than the smooth walls of the true pyramid we are familiar with today. The majority of these true pyramids were built around original stepped pyramids. This diagram shows the true pyramid of Maidum, *c.*2575 B.C., built around two internal stepped pyramids, the inner with seven and another with eight steps. An outer casing of limestone created the final smooth-walled structure.

Ships

Except for short distances, everyone and everything in Egypt travelled by boat.

The simplest form of boat, used for fishing expeditions or just crossing the river, was a kind of skiff, like a cross between a canoe and a punt. It was made of bundles of papyrus reeds tied together.

Bigger, sea-going ships were made of wood. As Egypt had few trees, the wood was imported, probably from Byblos on the coast of the Lebanon. It was from this port, in fact, that the Egyptians from about 2500 B.C. onwards imported wood for other purposes.

Archaeologists have discovered several Egyptian "boat yards". In one of these, close to the Great Pyramid of Giza, a large flat-bottomed boat, built of cedarwood, was found. It is about 43 metres (47 yards) long and 6 metres (6.5 yards) wide, and is made up of over 1,000 pieces of wood joined by wooden pegs or ropes made from a tough grass. It has a cabin, consisting of a wooden frame which would have been covered by a canopy, and six huge oars on each side. These were used for steering. The ship itself was towed by a fleet of small boats, since it has no mast and therefore no sail.

This was a river boat, probably a state barge used by the pharaoh. Sea-going ships had a mast, usually two poles meeting at the top and a single sail, as well as oars – twelve or more on each side besides steering oars at the stern (the rudder was still unknown).

In the reign of the great 18th-Dynasty pharaoh, Rameses III, Egypt fought a great naval battle against the "Sea Peoples" (perhaps Phoenicians), the first naval battle in recorded history. Pharaoh's warships were similar to merchant ships, but with some variations. The most notable addition was the ram at the bow, a hefty spike clad in metal for crashing into enemy ships.

These ships also had sails which could be furled (reduced in area) instead of just raised or lowered. They seem to have been very efficient vessels. Wandering around Mediterranean ports today, it is possible to see boats which in many ways are just as "primitive" as the warships of Rameses III built over 3,000 years ago.

Fishing boats on the Nile near Aswan. The scene has not changed greatly in 4,000 years.

40

Sculpture and Painting

To understand Egyptian art it is necessary to forget all modern ideas about art and artists. In modern Europe, the artist is an individual who is restricted in his work only by his own imagination and talent. He can paint or sculpt anything he likes.

The Egyptians had no word for "artist". Painters and sculptors were called craftsmen, the same word used for other workers in skilled jobs such as glassmaking or jewellery. The artist was just one member of a team of craftsmen who produced the finished work.

If the work were, say, a statue of a pharaoh, the first job was to cut a block of suitable stone. This in itself required training and experience. Having selected a likely piece, the mason made holes with his chisels and drove in wooden wedges, which he kept wet. In the hot sun, the wedges expanded and (if the mason had put them in the right places) cracked the rock.

Carving the statue out of the rock was not the job of an inspired artist – a Michelangelo or a Rodin. Several sculptors worked on it. One man specialized in cutting the hieroglyphics, for all official art had inscriptions. Another man made the eyes, yet another painted the finished statue. (All Egyptian statues were painted, to make them more lifelike, although in most cases the colours have long since disappeared.)

The finished product, whether it was a

Goldsmiths and jewellers at work, from a tomb painting.

Right: Head of Queen Nefertiti, in stone and plaster, painted. This is probably the most famous of all Ancient Egyptian works of art. The artist has caught the timeless elegance of the Queen, who is nonetheless a believable human being.

Far right: Battle scene carved in relief, from the Temple of Rameses II. To our eyes, such scenes are hard to follow.

statue or a scene carved in relief on a stone slab or a wall painting, was not meant to be an object of beauty. It had a purpose, and the artist worked to strict rules and conventions, which he learned during his training. We may think the result is beautiful, but the Egyptian artists did not think in those terms.

Nearly all the Egyptian art that has survived comes from temples and tombs. The statues and scenes in temples were there to fulfil a religious purpose. They represent Egyptian beliefs about life and the gods; they reflect the rigid ceremonies of worship, the idea of divine kingship, the relationship between gods and men, and the pharaoh's role as the link between them.

The art in tombs was intended to help the dead person on his way to the next world, and to provide him with all he needed when he got there. The paintings or sculptures on the walls would come alive, along with him, providing all the rules were followed and

the correct ceremonies were carried out.

Naturally, there was a lot of repetition. Even the keenest tourist, inspecting the endless scenes of battles, processions, feasts and so on in the Valley of the Kings at Thebes is likely to feel a sense of boredom after a time. But these art works were not meant to be seen like that. In fact they were seen by few people at all – only a few were allowed into the sanctuaries and tombs.

Not only are the scenes much the same, the subjects are portrayed according to fixed rules, which at first seem strange to our eyes. The most obvious example is the way human figures are presented. The head is seen from the side, the body from the front, and the legs again from the side. This was considered the best way to portray each part of the body. The fact that it is not how people look was not important.

Before work began, the area to be painted (or carved) was marked with a grid

The many, huge statues of Rameses II are identically posed. A different pose would have been a kind of blasphemy.

pattern. The picture was fitted strictly to the grid: a seated figure, for instance, took up a set number of squares in the grid. Although portraits were intended to be realistic, the strictness of the rules, which were so carefully followed by the artists, resulted in a certain sameness about the figures and faces.

The same convention which dictated that human figures should be shown as they are, not how they look as a whole, also governed other subjects. A building might be shown partly from the side and partly from the top. A lake in a painting appears as it would on a map, but the trees growing by it are painted as if seen from the ground.

Many of these ceremonial pictures tell a story, as in a comic. But they are not separated into panels, as a comic is. A farming picture shows what happens at different times of the year, but the pictures are run together in strips, or "registers", with no division between them. What looks like a chaotic sea battle with many ships taking part turns out to be a series of pictures of just two ships, illustrating different stages of the battle.

Many of the tomb pictures can be

regarded almost as lists. The dead man's possessions are represented with careful accuracy: his wives, his children, his fields of crops, his fruit trees and his animals. Here is a complete inventory of his estate.

Egyptian artists knew nothing of perspective – the way in which an impression of depth is made by painting distant objects smaller. Probably, they would not have been interested in such technical tricks. The nearest objects are usually placed at the bottom, farther away ones nearer the top. But there is no difference in scale. A cow 50 metres (54.6 yards) away is the same size as a cow 1 metre (1.09 yards) away.

When figures are shown in a different scale, it is a sign not of their position in the landscape but of their importance. Pharaoh appears as a giant, while his wife, poor thing, only comes up to his knee!

When painting a wall, a layer of plaster made from mud was put on first, to give a smooth surface. The grid pattern was marked out, probably by an apprentice, and the subjects were roughly sketched in, together with the hieroglyphics which explained the picture. In the final painting, sharp outlines were made in black and the colours painted in, usually without any attempt at "tone" or shading.

Brushes were made from reeds, with the ends frayed and cut to shape. Colours, in the form of thick paste, were made from various minerals: copper compounds made blue and green.

Colours were also dictated by convention. Osiris was always green, because green was the colour of regrowth and resurrection. Red was the colour of evil, and in the Old Kingdom, when hieroglyphics were painted in red, the artist drew a black line across them to take away bad magic.

Although they may not have thought of themselves as "artists", the painters and sculptors of Ancient Egypt certainly deserve that name for their skill alone. It is astonishing that they could produce such masterpieces with the simple materials then available. Enormous care and patience were required to make a monumental statue out of materials that were difficult to work with. In fact, experts are still uncertain how the Egyptian sculptor managed to put such a perfect, smooth finish on statues made out of such hard rocks as diorite.

Artists no less skilled than painters and sculptors made beautiful jewellery and small decorative objects like jars and mirrors. The quality of this work compares favourably with almost anything produced in later times. The Egyptian artist-

A beautiful glass flask, with looped decoration, made during the 18th Dynasty.

craftsman worked with a large variety of materials, from wood, clay and glass to crystal, marble and ivory, and he used many ornamental stones, like agate, jade, onyx, pearl and turquoise. Museums all over the world are full of the works of Egyptian artist-craftsmen. And yet how much has been lost! When we consider that what is left is probably much less than one per cent of the total produced, we get a better idea of the artistic wealth of Eygyptian civilization.

A magnificent example of Tutankamun's jewellery – a pectoral designed to be worn on the chest.

Index

Figures in *italics* refer to captions.

Abu Simbel *35*
Abydos 17
Alexander the Great 6, 17, 29
Amun 24, *24*, 26
Amun, Temple of 13
Amun-Ra 24, 25
Anubis 26, *26*, 27
army 32
Aswan 6, 33, 34, *40*
Aswan Dam 9
Atum 25

Bast *17*
British Museum 22, *28*

Cairo 6, *31*, 34, 37
calendar 29, 31
Canopic vases 28
cats 16, *17*
ceremonies 24, 42, 43
corn *see* grain

Deir el Medina *17*
demotic 29
Dendara *23*
desert 9, *10*, 11
Desert, Sinai 32
dynasties 6, 13, *22*, 27, *31, 32*, 33, 37, 40, *44*

flax 14
flood, annual 9, 26, 29, 38
floodwaters 9, 13

Geb 25
Giza 31, 37, *37*
glass 32, *32*, 41, *44*, 45
grain 12, 13, *13*
Greek 29

Hathor *8*, 25
Hatshepsut, Queen 33, *33, 34*
Heliopolis 24

hieratic 29
hieroglyphics *28*, 29, 41, 44
Horus *8*, 23, 25
Hyskos 6

Imhotep 24
irrigation 9, 14, *14*
Isis 25

Karnak 17, 26, 34

linen *see* flax
Luxor 17, 26, 34

Manetho 6
medicine 31
Mediterranean Sea 9, 11, 32, 40
Memphis 6, 17, *24*
Mesopotamia 8, 11, 29
Middle Kingdom 6
mummy 27, *27*, 28, 31

Napoleon 19
natron 27
Nefertiti, Queen *42*
New Kingdom 6, 11, 14, *15*, 17, 19, 34, 37, 38
Nile, river 6, *6*, 9, *9, 10*, 11, 14, *14*, 15, 29, 33, *40*
nomes 24
Nubia 11, *11*, 32, 33, 38
Nut 25

obelisk 35
Old Kingdom 6, 19, 24, *24*, 25, 34, 44
Osiris 17, 23, 25, *26*, 44

papyrus *17*, 29, 40
Persians 6
pharaoh 6, 8, 12, *18*, 22, 23, 24, *24*, 25, 27, *27*, 28, *31*, 33, 34, *35*, 37, *37*, 38, 40, 41, 42,

Pyramid, Great *31*, 37, 40
pyramids 6, 9, 12, 29, *31*, 34, 35, 37, *37*, 38

Ra 23, 24, 25
Rameses II *35, 37, 42, 43*
Rameses III 40
Red Sea 9, 33
Rosetta Stone *28*, 29

scribes 31, *31*, 38
Sebek 26
Seth 25
shaduf 14
silt 9
slaves 38
Sphinx *37*
Suez Canal 9
Sumerians 8, 29

taxes 9, 12, *12*, 13, 23, 24, 38
Thebes 13, 17, *17*, 33, 42
Thoth 25
Thutmose III 33
Tutankamun *18*, 27, *27*, 28, 37, *45*

Valley of the Kings 42
vizier 24